Remembering
Portland

Donald R. Nelson

TURNER
PUBLISHING COMPANY

Protection Engine Company volunteer firemen and apparatus (ca. 1880).

Remembering
Portland

Turner Publishing Company
4507 Charlotte Avenue • Suite 100
Nashville, Tennessee 37209
(615) 255-2665

Remembering Portland

www.turnerpublishing.com

Library of Congress Control Number: 2010902289

ISBN: 978-1-59652-615-0

Printed in the United States of America

ISBN: 978-1-68336-874-8 (pbk)

10 11 12 13 14 15 16—0 9 8 7 6 5 4 3 2 1

CONTENTS

Students pose in front of Central School on Sixth Street in 1865. The school was built in 1858. The Portland Hotel was later built on this block.

ACKNOWLEDGMENTS

This volume, *Remembering Portland,* is the result of the cooperation and effort of many individuals and organizations. It is with great thanks that we acknowledge the valuable contribution of the following for their generous support:

City of Portland Archives
Heathman Hotel
Portland Police Historical Society

We would also like to thank the following individuals for their valuable contribution and assistance in making this work possible:

Bill Failing
Tim Hills–Historian–McMenamins Pubs
Brian Johnson, Assistant Archivist, City of Portland Archives
Lori Kuechler, Executive Director, Portland Police Historical Society

And finally, we would like to thank those who contributed photographs from the following archives:

Mary Couch Robertson Butler Collection
Failing Family Archives
Gholston Collection
Frank Howatt
Nelson Photo Archive
Elaine Wiley
Yamhill County Historical Society

PREFACE

Portland, Oregon, has thousands of historic photographs that reside in archives, both locally and nationally. This book began with the observation that, while those photographs are of great interest to many, they are not easily accessible. During a time when Portland is looking ahead and evaluating its future course, many people are asking, How do we treat the past? These decisions affect every aspect of the city—architecture, public spaces, commerce, and infrastructure—and these, in turn, affect the way that people live their lives. This book seeks to provide easy access to a valuable, objective look into Portland's history.

The power of photographs is that they are less subjective than words in their treatment of history. Although the photographer can make subjective decisions regarding subject matter and how to capture and present it, photographs seldom interpret the past to the extent textual histories can. For this reason, photography is uniquely positioned to offer an original, untainted look at the past, allowing the viewer to learn for himself what the world was like a century or more ago.

This project represents countless hours of review and research. The researchers and writer have reviewed thousands of photographs in numerous archives. We greatly appreciate the generous assistance of the archivists listed in the acknowledgments of this work, without whom this project could not have been completed.

The goal in publishing this work is to provide broader access to sets of extraordinary photographs that seek to inspire, provide perspective, and evoke insight that might assist people who are responsible for determining Portland's future. In addition, the book seeks to preserve the past with adequate respect and reverence.

The photographs selected have been reproduced in vivid black-and-white to provide depth to the images. With the exception of touching up imperfections that have accrued with the passage of time and cropping where necessary, no changes have been made. The focus and clarity of many images are limited to the technology and the ability of the photographer at the time they were recorded.

The work is divided into eras. Beginning with some of the earliest known photographs of Portland, the first section records photographs from the nineteenth century. The second section spans the beginning of the twentieth century to World War I. Section Three takes a look at the city between the wars, and section Four moves from the World War II era to recent times.

In each of these sections we have made an effort to capture various aspects of life through our selection of photographs. People, commerce, transportation, infrastructure, religious institutions, and educational institutions have been included to provide a broad perspective.

We encourage readers to reflect as they walk in front of the Skidmore Fountain, along the Vera Katz Eastbank Esplanade, through Governor Tom McCall Waterfront Park, or through Washington Park. It is the publisher's hope that in utilizing this work, longtime residents will learn something new and that new residents will gain a perspective on where Portland has been, so that each can contribute to its future.

—Todd Bottorff, Publisher

Residence of former United States Senator and pioneer merchant, Henry W. Corbett, on Fifth and Taylor, circa 1877.

To the End of the Nineteenth Century

(1870s–1899)

Looking east from the Central School to the Portland Post Office, circa 1877. The Willamette River is visible in the distance.

Portland's combined Courthouse, Post Office, and Customs House in 1878. In the background is the expanded Central School.

Vigilance Hook and Ladder volunteer fire fighters with their apparatus in front of station on Fourth Street, circa 1880.

The Portland Police force poses for the camera in front of the City Jail in 1884.

The Portland Hotel, which opened in 1890, was to be built by Henry Villard, President of the Northern Pacific Railroad. Construction was halted in 1884 when financial difficulties arose. Portland businessmen banded together in 1888 to finance its completion. This construction view is from circa 1889, and shows the Seventh Street (Southwest Broadway) side of the hotel.

Joseph E. Penney's Gem Saloon on First Street in 1890 was a popular lunch spot for Portland businessmen. Adjoining the Gem was the cigar store of T. J. O'Brien.

George L. Baker, assistant manager of the Marquam Grand Opera House, sits next to the box office, circa 1896. It was in the Marquam Block, which was connected to the theater building. George L. Baker was Portland's mayor from 1917 to 1933.

Baseball team of the Portland Academy, circa 1896.

Encampment of Oregon National Guard soldiers at Irvington Race Track awaiting evaluation before becoming part of the Second Oregon Volunteers regiment that went to the Philippines in the Spanish-American War, 1898.

Late 1890s view on the Willamette River. The Madison Street Bridge is visible in the background.

The Skidmore Fountain during the 1890 flood. Completed in 1888, it was built from a $5,000 bequest from pioneer druggist Stephen G. Skidmore and the donations of others. The fountain was for horses and dogs; cups attached by chain to the fountain were for thirsty citizens. Etched on one side of the basin is the phrase "Good Citizens Are the Riches of a City."

Fire engine on barge at the northeast corner of Second and Oak streets during the flood of June 1894.

Fourth of July decorations at the Hose and Chemical 2 fire station on Southwest First Street in 1896.

Eastside waterfront, circa 1897. Many streets were built on trestles. Structures were built on pilings.

Fire Captain William R. Kerrigan, on the left, gets a shave, circa 1898.

Spanish-American War Parade on Fourth Street led by Portland policemen in 1898.

The Agriculture Building at the Lewis and Clark Centennial Exposition, circa 1905.

At the Turn of the Century

(1900–1919)

Theatrical troupe poses for an advertising photo in front of Hose 2 Fire Station on First Street, circa 1900.

Children (near political signs) in front of the Portland and OK coffee houses, circa 1900.

The Bear Pit at City Park, circa 1902. City Park was renamed Washington Park in 1912.

Police horse patrol policemen control the crowd at Sixth and Alder awaiting the parade for President Theodore Roosevelt, who after this event would dedicate the base of the Lewis and Clark Memorial at City Park, May 1903.

Boating on a stream in Portland, circa 1904.

The Union Avenue–Vernon streetcar at the end of the line, circa 1904.

R. C. Walworth and family grocery store on North Russell Street, circa 1905.

Part of the grounds of the Lewis and Clark Centennial and American Pacific Exposition and Oriental Fair of 1905.

Portland City Hall on Fourth Street, circa 1907. At this time the City Museum, which was a natural history museum, and the Oregon Historical Society, occupied a portion of this building.

The Portland Police baseball team at Vaughn Street Ballpark, circa 1908. Buildings from the 1905 Lewis and Clark Centennial Exposition are visible in the background.

St. Vincent's Hospital in northwest Portland, circa 1909.

August Storz grocery and provisions store on North Williams Avenue in 1910.

The Red Cross Ambulance Company's horse-drawn ambulance with nurses at the entrance to City Park in 1910.

Firemen's living quarters at Station 15, circa 1910.

Delivery wagons parked next to the Lang and Company Wholesale Grocery on First Street. The Skidmore Fountain and an office for the Western Union Telegraph Company are on the right, circa 1910s.

A view of wagons and businesses along Front Avenue, circa 1910.

Fire horses are harnessed to a fire engine, circa 1910.

At Union Station in northwest Portland, assorted vehicles await passengers for pickup and delivery to area hotels, circa 1910.

The employees and wagons of the Banfield Veysey Fuel Company pose next to Portland's Union Station, circa 1910.

Lownsdale Square of the Plaza Blocks, circa 1910. At the center is the Thompson Elk Fountain, which was given to the city by former Mayor D. P. Thompson.

An engineer and crew stand next to Engine no. 99 of the Oregon, Washington Railroad and Navigation Company at Union Station, circa 1910.

Members of the Harriman Club on a wagon decorated for a parade, pose next to the Y.M.C.A. at Sixth and Taylor streets, circa 1910.

Fire Chief David Campbell lost his life in the Union Oil Fire on June 26, 1911. Fearing that firemen were still in the building, he entered to save them. The building exploded and collapsed with him inside. Union Oil was located on East Water Street (today's Southeast Water Avenue).

Chief David Campbell's funeral on June 28, 1911, on Fourth Street. Honored and respected by many, he was referred to as "Our Dave," and people lined the street to observe his funeral procession. The hearse was pulled by his three favorite horses.

The Police Department's Pope Hartford patrol wagon parked beside the Portland Trust Bank in 1912.

Horse-drawn water wagon, circa 1912.

St. John's Volunteer Fire Department, circa 1914.

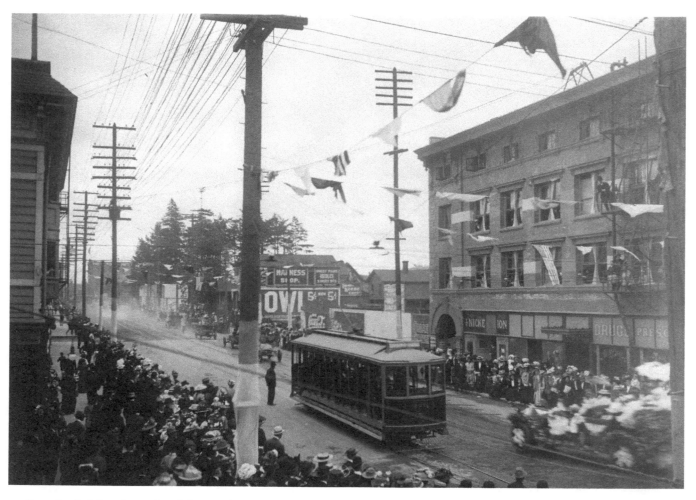

Rose Festival Parade on Grand Avenue in 1915. Roses took on a special meaning in the early 1900s. Portland became known as the Rose City.

Portland Police Band in 1915.

Office force of the Fire Department in 1915.

The Liberty Bell was on display on the Fourth Street railroad tracks next to the Multnomah County Courthouse in July 1915. The Liberty Bell was en route to the Panama Pacific Exposition in San Francisco. (In the background is Lownsdale Square of the Plaza Blocks.)

Broadway Bridge in 1915.

North Bank Station and Tanner Creek sewer repair in 1917.

Northeast Weidler Street during ice storm in 1917.

US National Bank on Sixth Street, circa 1918.

The new Post Office in northwest Portland, circa 1918.

The Library Association of Portland vacated its old overcrowded building and moved into the new Central Library at Tenth and Yamhill streets in 1913.

In this 1918 photograph, driver George Welch is seen pulling horse-drawn fire Engine no. 2 out of the station.

Fernwood Dairy, circa 1918 in southeast Portland at 15 Union Avenue (later SE Martin Luther King Jr. Blvd.). The business was in Harrington's Block, which was erected in the mid-1880s.

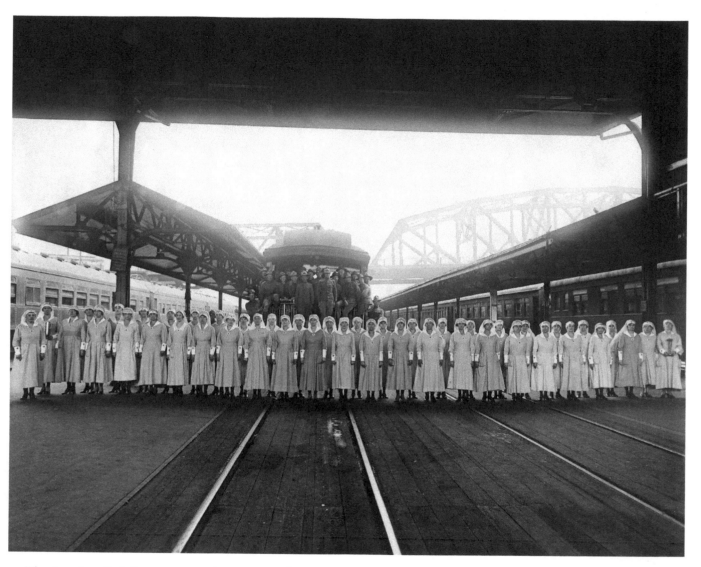

The American Red Cross canteen volunteers outside Union Station on September 28, 1918. These women met the troop trains and distributed magazines, candy, cigarettes, and other items to soldiers.

Airplanes at Mock's Bottom for 1919 war loan air show. Columbia University, today's University of Portland, is visible in the distance.

A Growing Metropolis

(1920–1939)

Construction crew for the Pacific Building at Sixth and Yamhill, circa 1924.

Peninsula Park Community House in North Portland in 1921.

Broadway from the Sovereign Hotel looking north, circa 1923. There were still a few old residences left in the downtown area.

Portland West Side Auto Camp, circa 1925, located on Terwilliger Boulevard.

Fire Rescue Squad no. 1 decorated for the Rose Festival, circa 1926.

The new Burnside Bridge, completed in 1926, is decorated for its opening.

Public Auditorium on Third Street and Market, circa 1926. During the Spanish Influenza epidemic of 1918, the year-old auditorium was put to use as a temporary hospital. A poster advertises the appearance of humorist Will Rogers. It was rebuilt in the 1960s and renamed the Civic Auditorium. Today it is known as Keller Auditorium.

Aviator Charles A. Lindbergh was in Portland to promote commercial aviation. His airplane, the *Spirit of St. Louis,* was on display at Swan Island Airport, September 14 and 15, 1927.

F. J. Howatt's Radiator Shop, in 1927, was in the new Multnomah Block on Morrison Street near Nineteenth Street. He advertised with this auto, "Headed Both Ways For Business."

The Winchester House Hotel at Third and Burnside in 1928.

Dredging the Willamette River for the new harbor wall in 1928. The old docks would soon be removed.

A diver plunges into the Willamette River during harbor wall construction in 1928.

Men relax and converse in the South Park Blocks, circa mid-1930s.

West Burnside from Fourth Street in 1930.

Lambert Gardens was a tourist attraction in southeast Portland for decades, circa 1930s.

Creston Park Swimming Pool in southeast Portland in 1930.

West Burnside at Sixth Street.

The St. John's Bridge under construction in 1930. The ferryboat beneath would soon be obsolete.

Fourth Street trestle in Southwest Portland in 1931, shortly before its removal.

Crews at the Hillside Drive construction in 1932.

Barbur Boulevard construction in Southwest Portland, 1933.

Market at NE 41st and Sandy Boulevard in 1934.

Handy Grocery at Southeast Thirteenth and Powell in 1934.

U.S. Veterans Hospital on Marquam Hill in southwest Portland, circa 1935.

Swimming pool at Sellwood Park in southeast Portland, 1935.

Vista Avenue Bridge and Reservoir 4 from Washington Park, circa 1935. The Jefferson Street entrance to Canyon Road curves under the Vista Avenue Bridge.

Southwest Oak Street in 1937.

The Piggly Wiggly Stop and Shop grocery store at Southeast 32nd and Burnside in 1937.

Southwest Stark Street looking west, circa 1939.

Auto Row on West Burnside in 1937.

Battleship *Oregon,* circa 1938. This view shows the ship at its new location, south of the Hawthorne Bridge that was developed into Battleship Oregon Memorial Park. The ship was relinquished to the government for scrap in 1942 and ended up as an ammunition barge. The mast was salvaged and today is part of the Battleship Oregon Memorial in Governor Tom McCall Waterfront Park.

Looking south on Northeast 82nd from the 1938 Soapbox Derby starting line.

North Broadway looking east to Interstate Avenue in 1939.

Southwest Washington Street and Fifth Avenue, circa 1939. The J. C. Penney Company is located on the right.

Street striping on Southeast Hawthorne in 1939.

The Northwest Tenth Avenue connection to the Lovejoy Viaduct in 1939, which carried traffic over the railroad yards.

Western Auto Supply Company at the intersection of West Burnside, Southwest Tenth Avenue and Southwest Oak Street, circa 1939.

The Dickson Drug Company in the Montavilla area of Portland at Southeast 80th and Stark in 1939.

The Speedball Cafe at Northwest Nineteenth and Burnside, circa 1939.

Aerial view of the Multnomah Athletic Club and Stadium, circa 1939.

View of a busy Southwest Fourth Avenue in 1940.

From the World War II Era to Recent Times

(1940–1970s)

The Santiseptic Company was located in the Schefter Building at Northeast Twentieth and Sandy Boulevard in this view from 1940.

Save-Rite Market, Liberty Tailors Cleaners, the 5, 10 & 25 Store, and the Jefferson Theatre featuring *The Mortal Storm* plus "Those Were the Days," are visible in this view of Southwest Jefferson at Eleventh, circa 1940.

Southwest First Avenue in 1940.

Vanport City, seen in this aerial view from 1943, was a planned community in North Portland built for shipyard workers.

Kaiser Company's Oregon Shipbuilding Plant on Swan Island in 1943. This location had previously been the site of the Swan Island Airport.

Gentleman hanging a sign reading "It's Patriotic to be Careful" during Safety Week in 1944.

The Hotel Medley at North Interstate and Albina avenues in 1945.

Rose Festival floats at Multnomah Stadium in June 1949.

Providence Hospital in northeast Portland, circa 1948.

In 1948, a service station and tire store shared the block at Southwest Fourth Avenue and Columbia with an old house and a hotel.

In May 1948, floodwaters of the Columbia River washed out a railroad fill in several places causing the Vanport community to be inundated with water. Apartment houses were ripped from their foundations. Although there was much devastation, loss of life was minimal.

A boy is carried through the 1948 Vanport floodwaters.

Council Crest streetcar at Southwest Fifth and Washington, circa 1949.

Portland mayor Dorothy McCullough Lee, center, at a new Blind School crossing signal in March 1950.

Rosy, a four-year-old elephant from Thailand, was brought to Portland for its zoo. She accepts a bouquet of roses at City Hall on September 26, 1953. Mayor Fred L. Peterson stands in the center of the group.

Southwest Sixth and Morrison in 1953.

President Dwight D. Eisenhower and his motorcade at Northeast 42nd and Prescott, a few weeks before the 1956 election.

Davis Pigeon Hole Parking Lot at Southwest Ninth and Oak in 1955.

Pittsburgh Paints store at Southwest Second and Salmon in 1956. Henry Black & Company is visible in the background.

Southwest Second Avenue at Oak Street in 1958.

Northeast Grand Avenue in the foreground, circa 1958, with the Sears buildings in view.

Mt. Hood Cafe and Union Station parking at Northwest Sixth and Irving in 1959.

Hilton Hotel under construction on Southwest Broadway in 1962.

Aerial view of the city in 1964. The South Park Blocks are seen on the left. An Urban Renewal area is on the right, in the foreground.

Southwest Fifth and
Madison, circa 1965.

City and County Mosquito Control Airplane crew, circa 1965.

Work on the Fremont Bridge center span in 1972.

First National Bank Tower in 1974.

Notes on the Photographs

These notes, listed by page number, attempt to include all aspects known of the photographs. Each of the photographs is identified by the page number, a title or description, photographer and collection, archive, and call or box number when applicable. Although every attempt was made to collect all data, in some cases complete data may have been unavailable due to the age and condition of some of the photographs and records.

Printed in the USA
CPSIA information can be obtained
at www.ICGtesting.com
JSHW072022140824
68134JS00042B/3745

9 781683 368748